THE MIRACLE OF SPIRITUAL SIGHT

COMPACT EXPOSITORY PULPIT COMMENTARY SERIES

THE MIRACLE OF SPIRITUAL SIGHT

Affirming the Transforming
Doctrine of Regeneration

DAVID A. HARRELL

© 2020 David A. Harrell

ISBN 978-1-7343452-9-2

Great Writing Publications, 425 Roberts Road, Taylors, SC 29687 www.greatwriting.org

Shepherd's Fire 5245 Highway 41-A Joelton, TN 37080 www.shepherdsfire.com

All Scripture quotations, unless stated otherwise, are taken from the New American Standard Bible® (NASB), Copyright © 1960, 1962, 1963, 1968, 1971, 1972, 1973, 1975, 1977, 1995 by The Lockman Foundation. Used by permission. www.Lockman. org All rights reserved.

No part of this publication may be reproduced, or stored in a retrieval system, or transmitted, in any form or by any means, mechanical, electronic, photocopying, recording or otherwise, without the prior permission of the publishers.

Shepherd's Fire exists to proclaim the unsearchable riches of Christ through mass communications for the teaching ministry of Bible expositor David Harrell, with a special emphasis in encouraging and strengthening pastors and church leaders.

Table of Contents

Books in this Series 6

Introduction 7

Regeneration 14

Regeneration and Spiritual Discernment 32

Regeneration and Self-Deception 56

Evidence of Regeneration 84

Endnotes 98

Books in this Series

Finding Grace in Sorrow: Enduring Trials with the Joy of the Holy Spirit

Finding Strength in Weakness: Drawing Upon the Existing Grace Within

Glorifying God in Your Body: Seeing Ourselves from God's Perspective

God, Evil, and Suffering: Understanding God's Role in Tragedies and Atrocities

God's Gracious Gift of Assurance: Rediscovering the Benefits of Justification by Faith

Our Sin and the Savior: Understanding the Need for Renewing and Sanctifying Grace

The Marvel of Being in Christ: Adoring God's Loving Provision of New Life in the Spirit

The Miracle of Spiritual Sight: Affirming the Transforming Doctrine of Regeneration

Introduction

On several occasions, I have had the opportunity to train pastors in Siberia and preach in Russian churches where almost every person had family members who were martyred for their faith in Christ at the hands of Stalin in the 1930s. I've seen the concrete walls where their relatives were required to stand to be shot, and I've heard many stories of the *gulags* (prison camps) where their Christian family members were sent to die because they were considered "enemies of the state."

But whenever I fellowship with our Russian brethren, they will inevitably share testimonies of God's saving grace that pursued them and drew them to Himself—stories of God's Spirit chasing after them, calling them with a call they could not resist. And whenever I reflect upon their testimonies, I'm reminded of my own, and many others I know and love who have experienced the same saving and transforming power of God's grace. I'm reminded of Peter's admonition to "sanctify Christ as Lord in your hearts, always being ready to make a defense to everyone who asks you to give an account for the hope that is in you" (1 Peter 3:15).

One such story is worth quoting; it's a story that will set the stage for the contents of this little volume, and it speaks of the power of God to instantaneously enable a person to turn to God in saving faith and be raised from spiritual death to spiritual life eternal. One of my Russian friends pointed me to this story as told by Andrea Wolfe (on staff with the CoMission office in Raleigh, North Carolina) and published by R. Kent Hughes under the title *The Hound of Heaven and Young Agnostic*. It reads as follows:

> In the 1930's Stalin ordered a purge of all Bibles and all believers. In Stavropol, Russia, this order was carried out with vengeance. Thousands of Bibles were confiscated, and multitudes of believers were sent to the gulags—prison camps—where most died, unjustly condemned as "enemies of the state."
>
> The CoMission once sent a team to Stavropol. The city's history wasn't known at that time. But when the team was having difficulty getting Bibles shipped from Moscow, someone mentioned the existence of a warehouse

outside of town where these confiscated Bibles had been stored since Stalin's day.

After the team had prayed extensively, one member finally mustered up the courage to go to the warehouse and ask the officials if the Bibles were still there. Sure enough, they were. Then the CoMissioners asked if the Bibles could be removed and distributed again to the people of Stavropol. The answer was "Yes!"

The next day the CoMission team returned with a truck and several Russian people to help load the Bibles. One helper was a young man—a skeptical, hostile agnostic collegian who had come only for the day's wages. As they were loading Bibles, one team member noticed that the young man had disappeared. Eventually they found him in a corner of the warehouse, weeping.

He had slipped away hoping to take a Bible for himself. What he did not know was that he was being pursued by the "Hound of Heaven." What he found shook him to the core. The inside page of the Bible he picked up had the handwritten signature of his own grandmother. It had been her personal Bible. Out of the thousands of Bibles still left in that warehouse, he stole the very one belonging to his grandmother—a woman, who throughout her entire life, was persecuted for her faith.

No wonder he was weeping—God had powerfully and yet tenderly made Himself known to this young man.[1] Such was his divinely appointed meeting with the sovereign Lord of the universe, the "Hound of Heaven" who had tracked him down to that very warehouse! Remember Jeremiah's words: "'Can anyone hide in secret places so that I cannot see him?' declares the Lord. 'Do not I fill both heaven and earth?' declares the Lord." (Jer. 23:24).

The "Hound of Heaven" and You

Jesus is truly the ever-present, all-seeing "Hound of Heaven." He can track us down wherever we're hiding! And once on the trail, He sets his heart with relentless zeal and undivided focus to the pursuit—a zeal that originally led Him directly to the ignominy of a Roman cross!

Choosing to leave behind the luxuries of Heaven's golden palaces and the unrivaled joy of the Father's presence, Jesus *willingly* descended into the ghetto of this present world—the realm of sin and Satan—in order to seek and to save that which was lost (Luke 19:10). Through the brutality of His suffering, climaxing in His voluntary death, He secured a startling triumph over hostile forces arrayed in battle against Him (and us). Having earned a once-for-all victory for His people, and having been resurrected to an indestructible life, He has returned to Heaven and His Father, where He *continues* to seek and to save that which was lost (Heb. 7:25). The young Russian man knows what this means. So does his grandmother. Do you?

You see, Jesus is still pursuing people through the message of the cross. The message of the cross rises above the myriad of voices and the noise in our culture, seizing our consciences by the throat and laying bare the depth of our selfishness and estrangement from God. If Jesus Christ was God Almighty incarnate, and His death was necessary to quell my rebellion, then I guess I know God's estimate of my sinfulness. "Oh wretched man that I am," says the apostle (Rom 7:24). But the good news is—for those who love Him— that all our filth has been transferred to Christ who willingly bore the guilt and pollution of our sin, death, and shame.

Thus, the message of the cross not only instructs me concerning the disastrous consequences of my rebellion, it also faithfully imparts the priceless knowledge of God's "other worldly," all conquering love—a love that changes "rebel" into "reconciled" and whose *intensity* can only be likened to a blood hound hot on the trail.

Like a major landmark *en route* to the place where God lives, the cross shows you and me the way home into the arms of our Father. It does not repel us from Him; on the contrary, it leads us confidently into His presence. Surely if He would suffer to this extent for us, then He must love us thoroughly.

In short, the cross calms my agitated, nervous heart and is like a smiling, gracious butler, who sees plainly that I am not clothed properly, but who nonetheless incessantly pleads with me to enter God's home where the real party never ends. Through the cross God Himself has provided the wardrobe appropriate for the festivities! He called our young Russian friend and now He calls you. Won't you come in?[2]

May this testimony of the regenerating power of the Spirit of God who has drawn us unto Himself in lovingkindness (Jer. 31:3) and caused us to be "born again to a living hope" (1 Peter 1:3) humble and excite our heart as together we examine the inscrutable mystery of regeneration.

1

Regeneration

I will give you a new heart and put a new spirit within you; and I will remove the heart of stone from your flesh and give you a heart of flesh. I will put My Spirit within you and cause you to walk in My statutes, and you will be careful to observe My ordinances.
Ezekiel 36:26–27

God's ancient promise to spiritually regenerate His covenant people Israel based upon a new and internalized covenant (Jer. 31:31–34) that would supersede the old covenant of the Mosaic law (2 Cor. 3:6) was a promise extended to all who believe (v. 18). The assurance of a radical inward renovation that would transform Israel's moral and spiritual nature corresponds precisely with the New Testament promise of regeneration for all believers (John 3:3–8; Rom. 8:2, 5, 9; Gal. 5:22; Titus 3:5–7; 1 Peter 1:22).

The Greek term for "regeneration" (*palingenesia*) refers to *a supernatural, instantaneous impartation of spiritual life to the spiritually dead characterized by both washing and renewal*. Paul used the term in Titus 3:5–7: "He saved us, not on the basis of deeds which we have done in righteousness, but according to His mercy, by *the washing of regeneration and renewing by the Holy Spirit*, whom He poured out upon us richly through Jesus Christ our Savior, so that being justified by His grace we would be made heirs according to the hope of eternal life" (emphasis mine).

This is what Jesus referred to in John 3 when He told Nicodemus, the great teacher of Israel, "You must be born again" (v. 7); "Truly, Truly, I say to you, unless one is born again he cannot see the kingdom of God" (v. 3); and again in verse 5 Jesus said, "Truly, truly, I say to you, unless one is born of water and the Spirit he cannot *(oú dunatai)* enter into the kingdom of God." The use of *oú dunatai* translated "he cannot" underscores the fact that *man is utterly powerless to enter into the Kingdom of God by any other means whatsoever*.

Jesus' use of the phrase "born of water and the Spirit" taken from Ezekiel 36:24–27 (which has nothing to do with water baptism) would have resonated with Nicodemus who undoubtedly knew the passage well. He would have understood that the terms "water" and "Spirit" were frequently used together in the Old Testament to symbolize spiritual renewal and cleansing, the very things Nicodemus craved!

> For I will take you from the nations, gather you from all the lands and bring you into your own land. Then I will sprinkle clean water on you, and you will be clean; I will cleanse you from all your filthiness and from all your idols. Moreover, I will give you a new heart and put a new spirit within you; and I will remove the heart of stone from your flesh and give you a heart of flesh. I will put My Spirit within you and cause you to walk in My statutes, and you will be careful to observe My ordinances.
> (Ezek. 36:24–27)

Jesus didn't give this fastidious keeper of the law an additional list of religious duties to perform that would somehow enable him to cooperate with God's grace because "It is the Spirit who gives life" (John 6:63). Man's soul is so corrupted by sin that nothing short of a total renovation can save him. All that man *is* and *does* is fundamentally offensive to our holy God, rendering man utterly unable to save himself. This is what makes the gospel such incredibly good news! In regeneration we are born "not of blood nor of the will of the flesh nor of the will of man, but of God" (John 1:13); man is entirely passive, wholly dependent upon the miraculous work of the Spirit. In light of this, we read in James 1:18: "In the exercise of His will He brought us forth by the word of truth."

Even as a child makes no contribution to his conception or birth in the physical realm—being totally dependent upon the activity of his parents—so, too, spiritually dead and depraved sinners make no contribution to their spiritual birth, being totally dependent upon the sovereign grace of God to raise them from spiritual death to life.

Pictures of Regeneration in Scripture

This effectual call of regeneration is pictured in the *future regeneration of Israel* where the Spirit of God breathes life into a valley full of dry bones (Ezek. 37:1–11), a stunning picture of man's natural state of depravity—nothing but dead, lifeless, bones, unable to respond to anything. But God promised, "Behold, I will open your graves and cause you to come up out of your graves, My people; and I will bring you into the land of Israel. . . . And I will put my Spirit within you and you will come to life and I will place you in your own land" (Ezek. 37:12, 14).

The same miracle is also pictured in the *account of Lazarus* in John 11 where Jesus stood at the tomb of his friend who had been dead for four days and then cried out, "Lazarus, come forth" (v. 43). "And the man who had died came forth" (v. 44).

We also see the Spirit giving life in Paul's comparison of regeneration to *God's creation of the world* recorded in 2 Corinthians 4:6: "For God, who said, 'Light shall shine out of darkness,' is the One who has shone in our hearts to give the Light of the knowledge of the glory of God in the face of Christ"—a reference to the Spirit's role in creation where He spoke the world into existence from nothing; when "God said, 'Let there be light'; and there was light" (Gen. 1:3). Dick Mayhew writes:

> In regeneration, God unites the external call of gospel preaching with his sovereign, effectual call unto new life. Into darkened and dead hearts he speaks the command, "Let there be light," and instantaneously births in us the light of eternal spiritual life where it had not existed.[3]

Because regeneration is that great bridge of grace that spans the infinite chasm between our depravity and the righteous demands of the law necessary to enter God's kingdom, the apostle Paul rejoiced, knowing God had empowered him to be a minister of "a new covenant, not of the letter but of the Spirit; for the letter kills, but the Spirit gives life" (2 Cor. 3:6).

Indeed, the "letter" of the law (referring to its legalistic, external requirements the Jews tried to obey to merit salvation) "kills." One violation of the covenant of God's law is punishable by death! So indeed, the law kills physically, and it also destroys joy, peace, and hope. Those burdened with the requirements of the Old Covenant lived under oppressive bondage. But that was the purpose of the law. It never had the power to redeem anyone from sin. Instead, its purpose was to demonstrate man's inability to live up to God's holy standard, cause him to acknowledge his sin and confess his impotence to merit salvation by his own works, and then to beg for undeserved forgiveness and grace resulting in salvation through Christ alone (Rom. 3:20; *cf.* Gal. 3:24). What a glorious truth: "the Spirit gives life" (2 Cor. 3:6b); indeed, He is the agent of regeneration, and in this we rejoice with exceeding joy!

The Miracle of Spiritual Sight

Regeneration was also pictured in John 9:1–12, when Jesus gave physical sight to the blind beggar. While this miracle was ultimately intended to validate Jesus' claim to be the Son of God and picture God acting in sovereign grace to save Israel who had been so influenced by Satan that they were blind to their guilt and bondage to sin, it also pictures the individual ruin of man's fallen nature rebelling against Jesus, the spiritual "light of the world" (John 8:12). The narrative describes Jesus taking the initiative to show mercy to "a man blind from birth" (v. 1). Those born blind from birth give no value to sight because they have no idea what they're missing. Likewise, the spiritually blind have no capacity to see the wretchedness of their condition or the imminent danger they are in; worse yet, they cannot see their desperate need for the Savior or the glory of His Person and work. None of us could have ever seen our sin or the Savior apart from divine initiative, because "there is none who seeks after God" (Rom. 3:11), so God must *seek* after us (Luke 19:10) and *save* us. Jesus said, "Unless one is born again, he cannot see the kingdom of God" (John 3:3).

As in the case of the blind beggar who was utterly destitute and helpless, every sinner is the same, spiritually speaking. Were it not for a merciful God who sought us out and stooped down to give us spiritual sight, we would still be walking in darkness.

It is a marvelous thing to consider how Jesus made clay with His saliva and applied it to the blind man's eyes. Perhaps this was a picture of original creation where God formed man out of the dust of the ground (Gen. 2:7) and was then preparing to create a new pair of eyes and all the organisms in the human body to make them function. For indeed, in order for eyes to see for the first time, there must also exist a pair of perfectly healthy retinas, corneas, and irises with their adjustable circular openings called pupils, which can expand or contract depending on the amount of light entering the eye. But that's not all. Physical sight would also require the creation of millions of nerve cells that had never been formed; cells that could perfectly transmit electrical signals of the optical images to the visual cortex in the brain. There would also need to be the creation of myriads of brain cells and neurotransmitters throughout the body that had never been formed because they were never needed. And if all this were not enough, first-time sight would also require the ability to suddenly process the flood of visual information so a person would be able to function accordingly.

Perhaps this simplistic physiological overview

of what would be required to create sight in a man born blind from birth will help us grasp the staggering implications of the miracle of the new birth—the miracle of spiritual sight in regeneration that makes us new creatures in Christ, and radically changes all that we are!

What happened next seems to symbolize Israel's rejection of the sent one: Jesus "said to him, 'Go, wash in the pool of Siloam' (which is translated, Sent). And so he went away and washed, and came back seeing" (v. 7). Here we witness the miracle of sovereign grace giving spiritual sight. "Go wash in the pool of Siloam"—how simple. Like the gospel: "Believe in the Lord Jesus, and you will be saved" (Acts 16:31). And will you notice, though the man could not *see*, he could *hear*, and this is how salvation comes to all of us: "Faith comes from hearing, and hearing by the Word of Christ" (Rom. 10:17). Our ears allow us to hear what our eyes cannot see. But one day we will behold and experience all that has been promised to us, making our "suffering of this present time not worthy to be compared with the glory that is to be revealed to us" (Rom. 8:18).

In Hebrew, the name *Siloam*, transliterates a Hebrew word *shiloah* that means "sent." The Old Testament reveals how King Hezekiah constructed a tunnel from the Gihon spring to the pool Siloam to guarantee a continual water supply in case they came under siege by the Assyrians. And what is truly fascinating to note is that during the Feast of Tabernacles where Jesus had just finished declaring Himself to be the living water (John 7:38) and the light of the world (John 8:12), the high priest drew water from the pool of Siloam, not knowing the "Sent One" was standing in their midst. Even as God's provision to deliver His people from their enemies came from the Gihon spring that flowed into the Pool of Siloam, Jesus, the Messiah of Israel, "the Sent One from God" (as He is often described in the New Testament) has come in fulfillment of that symbolism to deliver His people from their sins. But they would not receive Him!

In Isaiah 8:6 we read how King Ahaz and all of Judah "rejected the gently flowing waters of Shiloah (Siloam)" (Isa. 8:6), which typified God's help they refused to accept.

And here, they reject the very source of living waters sent from God! Yet in the mystery of sovereign grace, Jesus uses these same waters to bring help once again, to give this man sight—a living illustration of what could have happened to Israel in that day.

So, with Jesus taking all the initiative, this blind beggar went to the pool "and washed, and came back seeing" v. 7). Though he had not yet seen Jesus, he placed his faith in Him—an act demonstrated by his unquestioned obedience and personal testimony recorded later in the chapter where he is seen praising God.

Later we read of the indignation of the Pharisees. "They said to him, 'Where is He?' He said, 'I do not know'" (v. 12). Obviously, the man still hadn't seen Jesus with his new eyes. Then in verse 35 Jesus appears to him again after the man had been excommunicated from the Temple for his newfound faith in Christ: "Jesus heard that they had put him out; and finding him, He said, 'Do you believe in the Son of Man?' He answered, 'Who is He, Lord, that I may believe in Him?' Jesus said to him, 'You have both seen Him, and He is the one who is talking with you.' And he said, 'Lord, I believe.' And he worshiped Him" (vv. 35–38).

What a beautiful picture of divinely initiated faith that is always obedient faith—one that not only recognizes and worships the Lord Jesus Christ, but will also persevere, come what may. When a man is truly born again, he will make much of Christ; his constant testimony will be about Jesus, not himself. Charles Spurgeon wrote:

> If you are saved by Jesus, your star must set, but the star of Jesus must rise and increase in

brilliance till it becomes no more a star, but a sun, making your day, and flooding your whole soul with light. If we are saved Christ Jesus must and will have the glory of it. None on earth or in heaven can rival Jesus in the esteem of souls brought from darkness to light: he is everything to them.[4]

Regeneration Defined

I appreciate the definition of regeneration offered by a seventeenth-century Scottish pastor by the name of David Dickson who preached twenty-seven sermons on the subject in a town called Irvine, resulting in a mighty work of the Spirit in that realm. He defined regeneration this way:

> Regeneration is the work of God's invincible power and mere grace, wherein by his Spirit accompanying his Word he quickeneth a redeemed person lying dead in his sins and reneweth him in his mind, his will and all the powers of his soul, convincing him savingly of sin and righteousness and judgment, and making him heartily to embrace Christ and salvation, and to consecrate himself to the service of God in Christ all the days of his life.[5]

In his sermon *The Necessity of Regeneration*, Charles Spurgeon also captures the glorious mystery of the new birth, an unfathomable mystery that Jesus likened to the wind that blows: "The wind blows where it wishes and you hear the sound of it, but do not know where it comes from and where it is going; so is everyone who is born of the Spirit" (John 3:8). In light of this Spurgeon says:

> But what is it to be born-again? I have already said that I cannot tell you how the Spirit of God operates upon the unregenerate, making them to be new creatures in Christ Jesus. I know that He usually operates through the Word—through the proclamation of the Truth of the Gospel. So far as we know, He works upon the mind according to the laws of the mind by first illuminating the understanding. He then controls the judgment, influences the will and changes the affections. But over and above all that we can describe there is a marvelous power which He exerts which must remain among the inscrutable mysteries of this finite state, even if we can never comprehend it. By this power such a wondrous effect is produced that a man becomes a new man as much as if he had returned to his na-

tive nothingness and had been born-again in an altogether higher sphere! A new nature is created within him, although the old nature is not entirely eradicated. It will ultimately be destroyed, but it is not destroyed at first. Yet a new nature is born within the man, a nature which hates what the old nature loved, and loves what the old nature hated—a new nature which is akin to the Nature of God![6]

The natural man is incapable of seeing his need to be reconciled to God and wants nothing to do with it (1 Cor. 2:14). But with the miracle of the new birth, the sinner is given eyes to see his rebellion against God and ears to hear the truth of the gospel (Matt. 13:16–17). This is often called the effective (or efficacious) call of God, an operation of the Holy Spirit through the Word of God whereby individuals respond in faith and accept God's offer of salvation (Rom. 8:28–30; 1 Cor. 1:23–24; 2 Tim. 1:9; 1 Thess. 5:23–24; Eph. 1:18; 2 Peter 1:10). But the effective calling of God and regeneration seem to happen simultaneously, as Peter states, "For you have been born again not of seed which is perishable but imperishable, that is, through the living and enduring word of God . . . and this is the word which was preached to you" (1 Peter 1:23, 25). Similarly, James says, "In the exercise of His will He brought us forth by the word of truth" (James 1:18).

God's efficacious calling and regeneration results in the conviction of sin (Rom. 7:7), which in turn leads to repentant faith that *turns to Christ for salvation* and *turns away from sin and self-righteousness* (Acts 26:17–18; 1 Thess. 1:9). Because the natural man is dead in sin (Eph. 2:1–3) and thus unable to understand or accept the things of the Spirit of God (1 Cor. 2:14), repentant faith cannot occur apart from the new birth (John 1:13), a work in which sinners are entirely passive—for we "were born, not of blood nor of the will of the flesh nor of the will of man, but of God (John 1:13; *cf.* James 1:18; 1 Peter 1:3; John 3:3–8).

Essential Gospel Truths Neglected

These essential elements of the gospel, however, are seldom mentioned in the man-centered gospel of modern evangelicalism where the law of God has been eclipsed by a perverted understanding of the love of God—the new self-governing principle for Christian living that excuses and justifies all manner of sin and man's responsibility for it. John Fast writes,

This negation of the law of God has caused

the word "sin", along with any sense of its evil and guilt, to be dropped not only from common speech but from the speech and message of the vast proportion of professing Christianity as being too negative, judgmental, and unloving. Rather sin is given sanitized, psychologized, and respectable names. Instead of using biblical terminology and saying that a person is *"enslaved to various lusts and pleasures"* (Titus 3:3), and are *"indulging the desires of the flesh and of the mind"* (Eph. 2:3), we now say they have an addiction, a disease, or a disorder. Instead of being morally depraved, they are "sexually broken". People have, for the most part, eagerly accepted this more optimistic and naturalistic view of humanity that rejects the total depravity of man's nature.

At no point does a theology governed by emotion, sense, and sentiment rather than by facts and faith contend more with the clear teaching of Scripture than on the subject of sin, its guilt, and mankind's total depravity. Modern theology insists that the doctrine of man and sin taught by the Bible is incomprehensible to the present-day mind whose conceptions of man have been shaped largely by humanistic and naturalistic theories and the dogmas of secular psychology. Rather, we are told, people must be met at the level of their felt needs. It has become a maxim that people are really basically good and must be dealt with as "broken" and "hurting", not confronted with the truth that they are naturally depraved, evil, corrupt, and hostile to God and His word. This is a deadly error. God has not left it to each generation to determine their true condition and their greatest need. There is not one gospel for the first century, another for the tenth century, another for the eighteenth century, and another for our own.[7]

Without an awareness of the depths of our sin and the horror of the just punishment we deserve, salvation will never occur. Without an understanding of God's just wrath that abides upon deserving sinners (John 3:36), one cannot fully appreciate God's love for undeserving sinners. But with the miracle of regeneration, the Spirit quickens the dead to see their sin and the atoning work of Christ for what they are, and thus renews the mind, heart, and will. Yet the vast majorities of those who call themselves Christian today know nothing of this and therefore remain *unregenerate*. They have no awareness of their real need, resulting in a phony profession, a faith that cannot save, and an absence of spiritual discernment—topics we will now examine more closely.

2

Regeneration and Spiritual Discernment

But false prophets also arose among the people, just as there will also be false teachers among you, who will secretly introduce destructive heresies, even denying the Master who bought them, bringing swift destruction upon themselves.
2 Peter 2:1

It was a typical Sunday morning when I entered the worship center. The music was playing softly in the background while the saints began to gather. As always, the buzz of fellowship was sweet to my ears and even sweeter to my eyes as I looked into the faces of my precious flock and interacted with them personally. Every smile, every hug, every conversation bore witness to the power of God to bring together His people in mutual love and devotion to Him and one another. What an amazing sight! People from various parts of the world with varied ethnic backgrounds and a vast array of personal tragedies and triumphs, all coming together in unity to give praise to the one true God who had raised them from spiritual death to life and saved them by His grace.

But as I made my way through the flock, careful to give each family heartfelt attention, as every shepherd loves to do, my gaze suddenly fell upon a new couple I had never seen before. For the sake of anonymity, I'll call them Allen and Lisa. As I extended my hand of friendship, I remember saying to them, "Good morning. Welcome to Calvary Bible Church. I have not had the joy of meeting you." To which they replied, "No, this is our first time here, but we feel like we know you because we've been listening to your sermons online." Those are always encouraging words in our age where most so-called Christians will not endure sound doctrine but prefer to have their ears tickled by preachers who tell them what they want to hear rather than what God has said (2 Tim. 4:3).

Before we could pursue any further conversation, the music pastor asked everyone to take their seats and join together in singing a rousing hymn of praise as a call to worship. So I assured Allen and Lisa that we would chat more after church and that I would love to get to know them better; and at the close of the service we were able to do just that. Very quickly I learned that this was a couple that had journeyed through some very dark, even satanic valleys. While they didn't elaborate on all the details, what they did say, and the deep sorrow with which they said it, was enough to help me realize that God was up to something profoundly glorious in their lives — a story that would require several conversations and lots of coffee to fully tell.

Without getting into the details, suffice it to say that theirs was a story of lives once lived apart from Christ, of broken relationships and having to learn of the murder of their child at the hand of a depraved criminal, of the conviction of sin, of the transforming, saving and sanctifying grace of God, and of an unwitting association with a Word of Faith prosperity cult from which God rescued them after many years of involvement in the inner circles of leadership.

Like so many others, they were once very broken, fragile, and undiscerning people looking for help, babes in Christ in need of biblical discipleship and sound doctrine. With a church on virtually every street corner, they described how they chose one that seemed friendly and enthusiastic—a place where they assumed they would be loved, nurtured, and taught; a place where they could truly worship God and better understand how to walk with Him in humble obedience; a place where they could "grow in the grace and knowledge of our Lord and Savior Jesus Christ" (2 Peter 3:18). While their motives were pure, their lack of biblical knowledge crippled their spiritual discernment and made them easy prey for the false teachers that "owned the church."

For the first several years, Allen and Lisa enjoyed their new family, perceiving them to be Bible-believing Christians. They soon found ways to serve, and Allen was eventually ordained to preach by the hierarchy of their denominational system. Naturally, this catapulted him into the upper echelon of leadership, right next to the top man.

But as the years progressed, they began to struggle internally. What they were being taught and what they were expected to believe didn't match up with reality, and, as they studied their Bibles on their own and began to hear sound doctrine from faithful Bible expositors outside their circles, they began to question many things—but only privately. After all, they were told, "You don't question the man of God."

Their unanswered questions and suspicions started to grow exponentially as the Spirit of God began to open their eyes to the truth of Scripture and grant them discernment. As they became brutally honest with what they experienced and what they were learning from outside sources, they began to realize that the unbridled emotionalism and exaggerated testimonies of miraculous healings and material blessings during church services (many of which they knew were false) were incongruent with the reality of what they saw in the lives of the people during the week. The very real existence of blatant hypocrisy began to haunt them.

Notwithstanding what they knew to be true, they witnessed people filled with excitement and the confident assurance that if they had enough faith, they could unleash the power of God to achieve whatever they wanted. Over and over, they heard how God could be manipulated to make them prosperous, successful, and healthy. They were constantly hearing testimonies of how the Holy Spirit had empowered people to these ends, along with cherry-picked Bible verses used out of context to validate every experience. The congregation was told how the Holy Spirit and the angels were their "go getters" and how they could be commanded to do their bidding so they could be the "overcomers" God wanted them to be. They were shown how to just let themselves go emotionally and "speak in tongues" with no concern about what they were saying, because the Holy Spirit was giving them this language.

They were taught to use the phrase, "Say it and you can have it!" But they were stunned to see, for example, women in their church going into expensive clothing stores (knowing full well they couldn't afford anything) to lay hands on the garments they wanted and say, "I claim this in Jesus' name." They also began to see through the charade that if you didn't get what you wanted, it was because you either "didn't have enough faith" or because "God won't give you more than you can handle." Although Allen and Lisa began to see very clearly that there was no Scripture to support any of this, they were frightened to say anything in disagreement at the risk of being labeled "whores"—an epithet given to anyone who disagreed with the pastor, and especially those who left the church.

The sheer absurdity of having to avoid "negative statements" became increasingly intolerable to them. For example, Lisa once commented to a mother about the miserable condition of her sick little baby by saying compassionately, "Poor baby!" which elicited an immediate and very stern reprimand from the mother who said, "Don't say that! She's blessed, not poor!" And once when Allen said to the pastor, "I feel terrible today!" he was sternly rebuked: "No you don't! You're healed, you're blessed!"—a scenario that helped Allen see the frightening parallels of what he was being taught with the heresies of the Christian Science cult.

The Gullibility of the Unregenerate

While many other unbiblical deceptions could be cited with regard to Allen and Lisa's false church experience, the examples just described give ample evidence of the kinds of cleverly devised deceptions they endured, and what they were ultimately delivered from. But the purpose of this illustration is not to examine this apostate religious system that extends far beyond one church and includes hundreds of thousands of people worldwide. Rather, the purpose is to raise the question: *How can well-meaning, intelligent, professing Christians cling tenaciously to heresies that are so easily refuted biblically and are so demonstrably false experientially?* The answer is this: *They have never been born again and are therefore vulnerable to deception.*

Happily, because Allen and Lisa are truly regenerate, the Spirit of God dwells within them. He is their illuminating Guardian, the One who guides all believers into "all truth" (John 16:13) and empowers them to know "all things" (John 14:26; 16:13) pertaining to His revealed Word. He is the believer's resident lie detector that helps us persevere in the truth. The apostle Paul has written,

> Now we have received, not the spirit of the world, but the Spirit who is from God, so that we may know the things freely given to us by God, which things we also speak, not in words taught by human wisdom, but in those taught by the Spirit, combining spiritual thoughts with spiritual words.
> (1 Cor. 2:12–13)

John explained how those who embrace grievous and obvious heresies prove they were never born again (1 John 2:19): "But you have an anointing from the Holy One, and you all know" (v. 20). He went on to say, "As for you, the anointing which you received from Him abides in you, and you have no need for anyone to teach you; but as His anointing teaches you about all things, and is true and is not a lie, and just as it has taught you, you abide in

Him (v. 27); and "by this we know that we abide in Him and He in us, because He has given us of His Spirit" (1 John 4:13).

Not a week goes by that I don't hear someone say, "How can anybody believe that stuff?" At times the subject pertains to politics, for indeed many policies put forth by our political leaders are unspeakably evil and absurd, often based upon presuppositions that are easily refuted by facts. But the most common theme that foments incredulity pertains to unbiblical and irrational beliefs held by professing Christians. Frankly, anyone who believes the health-and-wealth promises of the Word of Faith movement's deceptive prosperity gospel has no basis to claim he or she has been "born of the Spirit" (John 3:6) or "brought forth by the word of truth" (James 1:18). And that gospel truth is simply this: *God has provided a way for sinners to be reconciled to Himself through faith in the Lord Jesus Christ who died vicariously to save sinners from the penalty, power, and presence of sin.* Anyone who preaches a gospel that is even slightly contrary to this doctrine of salvation proclaimed by Jesus Christ and the apostles "is to be accursed" (Gal. 1:8). Moreover, those who peddle a false gospel for profit are "false teachers" who "secretly introduce destructive heresies, even denying the

Master who bought them, bringing swift destruction upon themselves" (2 Peter 2:1).

The charismatic obsession with the supposed gifts and power of the Holy Spirit rather than the person and work of Christ is sufficient evidence to demonstrate that something is terribly wrong with that brand of pseudo-Christianity, yet there are increasing numbers of people who accept it enthusiastically. The watching world laughs as they witness fake healings and the bizarre behaviors of frenzied emotionalism, such as nonsensical babbling, uncontrollable laughter, and falling on the floor claiming to be "slain in the Spirit." The idiotic antics and blasphemous beliefs of the prosperity preachers (both male and female) makes one wonder what kind of delusional force is at work in them—and in those who follow them.

Only Satan and his minions would cause someone to prostrate himself upon the grave of a deceased preacher to soak up the "anointing" from his corpse—a practice known as "grave-sucking."[8] Only a person bereft of the indwelling presence of the Holy Spirit could possibly believe that seizures, hypnosis, hysteria, and being "slain in the Spirit" are works of the Holy Spirit. We've all seen meetings that can be likened to a religious version of professional wrestling where the atmosphere is electric with excitement and everyone is enjoying the show. The problem is, they don't see it as a show; they think it's real!

What drives this kind of gullibility? Furthermore, what causes people who claim to be Christians to feel as though they must look for something else after their supposed conversion because they're empty inside? The answer is this: *They are unregenerate.* Eric Alexander has written: "I am sure that one of the reasons people are looking for additional, secondary thrills offered at some future stage in their religious experience is that they have devalued the initial work of grace."[9]

The renewed heart is a radically new heart that finds the majesty of Christ's saving grace and transcendent glory so irresistibly compelling that everything else in life pales in comparison. It is a heart that counts "all things to be loss in view of the surpassing value of knowing Christ Jesus my Lord" (Phil. 3:8). There is nothing in the human experience that can compare to the soul-satisfying joy of a believer's intimate spiritual union with the Lord Jesus. Charles Spurgeon said it best: "There is no joy in this world like union with Christ! The more we can feel it, the happier we are, whatever our circumstances."[10]

The Unseen Enemy

It is also important to remember that even genuine believers can be *deceived* for a while, like the immature saints Paul described in 1 Corinthians 3 who were ruled by their flesh more than the Spirit, "men of flesh . . . infants in Christ" (1 Cor. 3:1). For example, it is not uncommon to see carnal babes in Christ temporarily populating apostate evangelical denominations that not only support, but also promote political movements and beliefs that are blatantly unbiblical. As immature believers, Allen and Lisa were temporarily deceived as we all have been in various ways.

Jesus warned that "false Christs and false prophets will arise and will show great signs and wonders, so as to mislead, if possible, even the elect. Behold, I have told you in advance (Matt. 24:24). Indeed, "many deceivers have gone out into the world" (2 John 7) and their lies can be easily spread through electronic media like radioactive particles after a nuclear detonation. Peter warned: "But false prophets also arose among the people, just as there will also be false teachers among you, who will secretly introduce destructive heresies" (2 Peter 2:1). Paul described them as "holding to a form of godliness, although they have denied its power" (2 Tim. 3:5), and then he added this command: "Avoid such men as these. For among them are those who enter into households and captivate weak women weighed down with sins, led on by various impulses, always learning and never able to come to the knowledge of the truth" (vv. 6–7).

But the primary source of deception is the *unseen enemy*, Satan himself, the father of lies (John 8:44), "the prince of the power of the air . . . the spirit that is now working in the sons of disobedience" (Eph. 2:2). The New Testament record is filled with warnings concerning the devil's implacable malice toward Christ and His church—a rage that gives rise to his ingenious demonic deceptions that cause people to believe lies, "the mystery of lawlessness . . . already at work" in the world (2 Thess. 2:7; *cf.* Eph. 6:12). To be sure, he is "the god of this world" who "has blinded the minds of the unbelieving, that they might not see the light of the gospel of the glory of Christ, who is the image of God" (2 Cor. 4:4). Paul's somber warning should grip us all: "But the Spirit explicitly says that in later times some will fall away from the faith, paying attention to deceitful spirits and doctrines of demons, by means of the hypocrisy of liars seared in their own conscience as with a branding iron" (2 Tim. 4:1–2).

Sadly, however, many professing evangelicals are indifferent to the existence of Satan and his strategies to destroy the true church in general, and their lives in particular. Few take seriously the warning to

> Put on the full armor of God, so that you will be able to stand firm against the schemes of the devil. For our struggle is not against flesh and blood, but against the rulers, against the powers, against the world forces of this darkness, against the spiritual forces of wickedness in the heavenly places. Therefore, take up the full armor of God, so that you will be able to resist in the evil day, and having done everything, to stand firm.
> (Eph. 6:11–15)

The moral freefall and spiritual darkness in America is the inevitable consequence of unchecked human depravity and satanic blindness that have been able to thrive in a religious climate where the spiritual salt of evangelicalism has lost its savor and the light of the gospel has been all but extinguished by those who prefer darkness rather than light.

Satanic Influence Historically

It was no mere coincidence that at the very birth of the church, the Spirit of God underscored the grave danger of satanic influence by revealing Satan's nefarious activities in two of its members. This chilling scene is recorded in Acts 5:3 when Peter said, "Ananias, why has Satan filled your heart to lie to the Holy Spirit." The subsequent judgment against this man and his co-conspirator wife, Sapphira, caused "great fear [to come] upon the whole church, and upon all who heard of these things" (v. 11).

But there is little fear in the church today. The sin of hypocrisy and the power of Satan to animate it within people who are superficially attached to the church (like Judas Iscariot) are seldom even seen, much less dealt with, in modern evangelicalism. Far too often, we hear a misguided cry for *ecclesiastical unity (ecumenism).* But this can only be accomplished at the *expense of sound doctrine*—what Paul defined as "the unity of the faith, and of the knowledge of the Son of God" (Eph. 4:13). This has produced a mongrel church bereft of spiritual discernment and power. Much of modern evangelicalism has become nothing more than an amorphous entity controlled by the prevailing winds of culture rather than by the Word of God.

Over the course of my lifetime, I have witnessed

a frightening "openness" mentality that has now evolved into a full-blown ecumenical ethos that cannot co-exist with the New Testament church whose spiritual authenticity can be seen most clearly in the Protestant church of the Reformation. Evidence of this can be seen historically in various movements around the world, perhaps most notably in the Billy Graham Evangelistic Association. Graham said this:

> I feel I belong to all the churches. I am equally at home in an Anglican or Baptist or a Brethren assembly or a Roman Catholic church. . . . Today we have almost 100 percent Catholic support in this country. That was not true twenty years ago. And the bishops and archbishops and the Pope are our friends.[11]

For the most part, contemporary evangelicalism has been deceived by the satanic philosophies of postmodernism that rejects the concepts of absolute or moral truth and considers tolerance of all religious and cultural issues to be a manifestation of Christian love. "People of faith," as religious people are often called, prefer *conversations* to *proclamations*—despite God's mandate to the contrary (Matt. 28:19–20; 1 Tim. 4:13; 2 Tim. 2:2; 4:2; Titus 2:1). Avant-garde evangelicals consider biblical preaching to be passé, authoritarian, and sectarian. They prefer motivational speeches, conversational sermonettes, and dialogues between various faith communities—modes of communication that value *experience* over *truth* and tolerance of all views (except biblical Christianity), no matter how absurd or contradictory. Because of this, any attempt to "contend earnestly for the faith" (Jude 3) is considered to be an unacceptable act of arrogance and intolerance, contrary to the humility and love of Christ.

The command to "examine everything carefully; hold fast to that which is good; abstain from every form of evil" (1 Thess. 5:20–22) has therefore fallen on deaf ears. Because few pastors today are willing to confront and attack error (2 Cor. 10:3–5), most churches are not "the household of God . . . the pillar and support of the truth" (1 Tim. 3:15). Instead, they have become "the dwelling place of Satan . . . the pillar and support of deception." Iain Murray refutes this modern "openness" writing:

> Instead of believers in the apostolic age being directed to listen to all views "with an open mind", they were told how to "test the spirits, whether they are of God" (1 John 4:1). For there are "deceiving spirits and doctrines of demons" (1 Tim. 4:1); false teachers "who will

secretly bring in destructive heresies" (2 Peter 2:1). There are words which "spread as a cancer" (2 Tim. 2:17).

Allen and Lisa's testimony is one of millions that confirm Satan's ability to deceive those who embrace the blasphemous heresies of the Word of Faith cult. Notwithstanding the fact that there are many other professing evangelicals that would categorically reject such extreme doctrinal perversions and wholly affirm (at least in principle) the doctrinal truths of historic Protestant orthodoxy, many do, however, embrace the values and priorities of contemporary culture so strongly that they cannot be distinguished from the world—perhaps the most ingenious of all Satan's strategies to deceive.

As a result, countless people have responded to a watered-down gospel carefully crafted to attract virtually anyone regardless of what he or she believes about the glory of the Person and work of the Lord Jesus Christ. Churches are then populated with unbelievers who "did not receive the love of the truth so as to be saved" (2 Thess. 2:10); who "[do] not accept the things of the Spirit of God" and "cannot understand them, because they are spiritually appraised" (1 Cor. 2:14). This was at the heart of the apostle Paul's great concern for the church at

Corinth when the people there were being taught a different gospel, causing him to say, "But I am afraid, lest as the serpent deceived Eve by his craftiness, your minds should be led astray from the simplicity and purity of devotion to Christ" (2 Cor. 11:3). Would that all churches share such a concern.

With churches filled with people who are "Christian" in name only, it is little wonder that "they will not endure sound doctrine . . . and will turn away their ears from the truth, and will turn aside to myths" (2 Tim. 4:3–4). Bottom line, much of the church today is made up of unbelievers. This is why we witness such an abysmal lack of discernment in ostensibly evangelical churches that are content to live in a fool's paradise of satanic deception. It is frightening to witness churches that are "open" to the false doctrines of Roman Catholicism and the Word of Faith cult, or actually promote unbiblical ideologies like the LGBTQ agenda, radical feminism, and progressive liberal (often Marxist) politics. And what is most telling is that even the gentlest rebuke is met with hostility so fierce that it can only be accurately described as demonic.

Under the heading *Satan and The Gospel*, the eighteenth-century Scottish churchman Horatius Bonar (1808–1889) offers some powerful and compelling insights regarding Satan's diabolical opposition to the purposes of God that we would do well to consider with utmost solemnity. He writes:

> Let us mark how, in these days of ours, he works, and tempts, and rages: He comes as an angel of light, to mislead, yet pretending to lead; to blind, yet professing to open the eye; to obscure and bewilder, yet professing to illuminate and guide. He approaches us with fair words upon his lips: liberality, progress, culture, freedom, expansion, elevation, science, literature, benevolence, nay, and *religion* too. He seeks to make his own out of all these; to give the world as much of these suits his purpose, as much as will make them content without God, and without Christ, and without the Holy Ghost. . . .
>
> He sets himself against God and the things of God in every way. He can deny the gospel; or he can dilute the gospel; or he can obscure the gospel; or he can neutralize the gospel; just as suits his purpose, or the persons with whom he has to do. His object in regard to the gospel is to take out of it all that makes it glad tidings to the sinner; and oftentimes this modified or mutilated gospel which looks so like the real, serves his end best; for it throws men off their guard, making them suppose

that they have received Christ's gospel, even though they have not found in it the good news which it contains.

He rages against the true God—sometimes openly and coarsely, at other times calmly and politely—making men believe that he is the friend of the truth, but an enemy to its perversion. Progress, progress, progress is his watchword now, by means of which he hopes to allure men away from the old anchorages, under the pretext of giving them wider, fuller, more genial teachings. He bids them soar above creeds, catechisms, dogmas, as the dregs of an inferior age, and a lower mental status. He distinguishes, too, between theology and religion, warmly advocating the latter in order to induce men to abandon the former. He rages against the divine accuracy of the Bible, and cunningly subverts its inspiration by elevating every true poet and philosopher to the same inspired position. So successfully has he wrought in disintegrating and undermining the truth, that there is hardly a portion of it left firm. The ground underneath us is hollow; and the crust on which we tread ready to give way, and precipitate us into the abyss of unbelief.[12]

The Inevitable Consequence of Worldliness

As Satan sows tares among the wheat, much of evangelicalism has taken on a whole new image. Its obsession with church growth at the expense of sound doctrine has shifted the church's purpose as the proclaimer and protector of divine truth (1 Tim. 3:15; Titus 2:1, 15) into an amorphous amalgam of social services, pseudo-Christian entertainment, prosperity hustling, and political activism. Worse yet, rather than heeding the command to come out and be separate from the world (2 Cor. 6:14–18), the church has become more like the world, a phenomenon that produces success in the eyes of man, but triggers judgment in the eyes of God. Iain Murray describes this dynamic:

> . . . evangelicals, while commonly retaining the same set of beliefs, have been tempted to seek success in ways which the New Testament identifies as "worldliness". Worldliness is departing from God. It is a man-centered way of thinking; it proposes objectives which demand no radical breach with man's fallen nature; it judges the importance of things by the present and material results; it weighs success by numbers; it covets human esteem and wants no unpopularity; it knows no truth for

which it is worth suffering; it declines to be a "fool for Christ's sake". Worldliness is the mind-set of the unregenerate. It adopts idols and is at war with God. . . . It is professing Christians who are asked, "Do you not know that the friendship of the world is enmity with God?" (James 4:4) and are commanded, "Do not love the world", "keep yourselves from idols" (1 John 2:15, 5:21). Apostasy generally arises in the church just because this danger ceases to be observed.

The consequence is that spiritual warfare gives way to spiritual pacifism, and, in the same spirit, the church devises ways to present the gospel which will neutralize any offence. The antithesis between regenerate and unregenerate is passed over and it is supposed that the interests and ambitions of the unconverted can somehow be harnessed to win their approval for Christ. Then when this approach achieves "results"—as it will—no more justification is thought to be needed. The rule of Scripture has given place to pragmatism. The apostolic statement, "For if I still please men, I would not be the servant of Christ" (Gal. 1:10), has lost its meaning.[13]

Murray's statement, "the antithesis between regenerate and unregenerate is passed over," summarizes the primary focus of this book. While Satan employs a vast array of ingenious deceptions, there is perhaps none more diabolical than his ability to blur the line between those who are truly born again and those who are not, the subject of the next chapter.

3

Regeneration and Self-Deception

Not everyone who says to Me, "Lord, Lord," will enter the kingdom of heaven, but he who does the will of My Father who is in heaven will enter.
Matthew 7:21

Spiritual apostasy within the ranks of evangelicalism has caused it to be on a precipitous decline for many years, especially since its partnering with theological liberalism in the nineteenth century—a system that essentially denies the inspiration and authority of Scripture and argues that Christianity is more defined by feelings and experience than adherence to certain doctrines. As a result, the very definition of a Christian has become so blurred that virtually anyone who has fond feelings for the benevolent aspects of the teachings of Christ can be considered a Christian. Historically, this spawned the ecumenical movement that believes Christianity has nothing to do with embracing fundamental biblical truths essential to salvation, but is rather defined by people who love God and love one another. While commitment to unity would appear on the surface to be a commendable cause, unity at the expense of truth is a damning deception. As Iain Murray states,

> Liberalism has had all the marks of the false prophet. It promised a great growth in light and Christian influence for the nations where it was adopted. Instead there has been spiritual desolation. This is exactly what we who believe Scripture should have expected.[14]

Wherever the essential doctrines of soteriology are discarded as the ancient relics of fundamental obscurantists who cause unnecessary division, the true gospel will be replaced by a false gospel and the church will be populated with unbelievers. We all know people who affirm the gospel and yet remain strangers to its saving and sanctifying power. This was true of a good friend of mine who was saved out of a lifetime of regular church attendance in a liberal church where he never heard the true gospel but who was gloriously saved and has now been a faithful pastor for number of years. Here's what he said:

> Having lived most of my life in the so-called "Bible Belt," I have met and known scores of people who profess to be Christians, yet in their daily lives have been indistinguishable from those who have never made such a profession. In fact, I myself used to be such a person. I have lived both sides and seen the fallacy of one and the truth of the other.
>
> Such people as I once was rarely read their Bibles, much less know them. They take no delight in talking about the things of the Lord. Their lifestyles are as worldly and self-indulgent as their incomes will allow, and oftentimes more than they will allow. Their minds are set on and preoccupied with earthly things. In their dress they take their cues from the culture, or are driven by personal preference rather than biblical principles, and are just as immodest, provocative, ostentatious, and sensual as the world.
>
> They allow the culture to dictate the standard of modesty and morality, and what is appropriate and inappropriate. They watch

the same ungodly movies, listen to the same music, are influenced by and follow the same fads and trends, and reflect the same values, priorities, thinking, and reasoning of the culture. Their speech is often coarse and profane. Their social media platforms are shallow, vain, self-promotional, complement-seeking, and narcissistic. They have no devotion or love for spiritual truths and biblical principles, especially if they contradict some preference or presupposition, or require an alteration in their thinking, values, beliefs, and lifestyles, and to forsake some cherished lust and sin.

Their giving to the work of the Lord is sporadic, self-serving, and minimal at best, with virtually no inconvenience to their overall lifestyle. They are not only utterly incapable of discerning truth from error, the clean from the unclean, the holy from the profane, and the fruit that is from the spirit of the world from the fruit that is of the Spirit of God, but they are completely indifferent toward them. They can listen to what is good and true, and to what is bad and heretical, without any discrimination.

But for all of this they are quite certain they will go to heaven when they die. If you ask them what is the basis for this confidence, they will tell you that many years ago they accepted Jesus as their Savior and invited Him into their heart, and "once saved, always saved" is their comfort and assurance. But the sign and evidence that someone is truly regenerate is not some empty prattling about how secure they are once they made a profession of faith, but "that though you were slaves of sin, you became obedient from the heart to that form of teaching to which you were committed" (Rom. 6:17).[15]

Perhaps the most chilling statement in all of the Bible is recorded in Matthew 7:21 where Jesus says, "Not everyone who says to Me, 'Lord, Lord,' will enter the kingdom of heaven." What a dire warning to the masses of people who claim to be Christians but are not. What a horrifying climax to a life of self-deception when those who have professed Christ with their lips but not with their life will stand before Jesus Christ as their Judge and Executioner, but not as their Savior and "Lord" as they claimed. A day when "the One who has been appointed by God as Judge of the living and the dead" (Acts 10:42) will strip away the external robes of hypocrisy and expose the naked truth of a soul that was "Christian" in name only.

Jesus' frightening prediction should cause everyone who calls Jesus "Lord" to make a careful, unbiased, and brutally honest evaluation of his or her heart. As the apostle Paul warned, "Test yourselves to see if you are in the faith; examine yourselves! Or do you not recognize this about yourselves, that Jesus Christ is in you—unless indeed you fail the test?" (2 Cor. 13:5).

The Broad and the Narrow Way

In Matthew 7, Jesus begins to address these dangers by cautioning believers to use righteous discernment when judging others (vv. 1–2; *cf.* John 7:24). Then He warns of the hypocrite who is prone to see the speck in another man's eye but not the log in his own (vv. 3–4)—a reference to professing Christians who cannot perceive who they really are. Jesus says in Matthew 6:22–23, "The lamp of the body is the eye; if therefore your eye is clear, your whole body will be full of light. But if your eye is bad, your whole body will be full of darkness. If therefore the light that is in you is darkness, how great is the darkness!" Hypocrites cannot see the light of truth because the internal corruption of their very nature emanates darkness from within them, causing them to walk in darkness, which they perceive to be light.

Jesus then presses His followers to choose between two options, both claiming "This way to heaven!" First, He asks them to choose between two gates: the *narrow* and the *wide*, and then commands them to "Enter through the narrow gate: for the gate is wide and the way is broad that leads to destruction" (v. 13). The term "narrow" (*stenos*) comes from a root word meaning "to groan" and is used to describe a compressed or restrictive gate that is not entered with ease. John Nolland writes:

> Matthew has probably chosen the imagery of narrowness to suggest the constriction of one's choices involved in taking the challenge of Jesus' teaching: there is a very sharply defined mode of entry. The narrow gate throws up images of the need to make a choice which is not obvious (this is not where the crowd is going to go), to be attentive to where the gate is located, perhaps to experience the discomfort of squeezing through a narrow space.[16]

The gate of authentic saving faith requires someone to squeeze through without the excess baggage of self-righteousness. It requires the recognition of spiritual bankruptcy, of being consumed with guilt over sin and fully aware of the judgment deserved for having violated the laws of a holy God. When a person truly comes to saving faith, he or she will experience the intense pressure of a conscious choice to renounce the old self and put on Christ—a determined, purposeful decision requiring strenuous effort. This, of course, is the opposite of the "easy-believism" and "decisionism" of altar call revivalism where calculated and emotionally induced outward acts (like walking an aisle and repeating a prayer) are considered to be evidence of regeneration rather than a changed life.

We see the same emphasis in Jesus' response to the question, "Lord, are there just a few who are being saved?" He answered, "Strive to enter the narrow door, for many, I tell you, will seek to enter and will not be able" (Luke 13:23–24). "Strive" (*agonizomai*) signifies an intense exertion against conflict, indicating that this is not a gate a man enters with ease, nor will it be a wide gate that attracts the masses. Instead, it will be a gate that one must enter deliberately with determined effort and all alone.

This is the gate of genuine conversion, entered by the overwhelmed, the helpless, the hopeless, the one that cries out like the publican, "Have mercy upon me the sinner!" (Luke 18:13) This is the gate of *self-denial*, not *self-fulfillment*—a gate that requires a man to count the cost of discipleship, discard self-will, jettison self-righteousness, reject selfish ambitions, and become the willing slave of his Savior and King. Jesus put it this way: "If anyone wishes to come after Me, let him deny himself, and take up his cross, and follow Me. For whoever wishes to save his life shall lose it; but whoever loses his life for My sake shall find it" (Matt. 16:24–25). To "deny" literally means to renounce yourself, to be repulsed by your sin and all the ways it has corrupted your life and made God your enemy—a radical departure from the *man-centered gospel* of self-fulfillment and self-indulgence or the heretical *social justice gospel* that focuses on *how to be delivered from the social injustice of man* rather than *how to be delivered from the righteous justice of God*. Central to entering the narrow gate is a terrifying conviction of sin and a clear understanding of the message of Acts 4:12: "And there is salvation in no one else; for there is no other name under heaven that has been given among men by which we must be saved."

In addition to this, Jesus warns, "For the gate is small, and the way is narrow that leads to life, and few are those who find it" (Matt. 7:14). The reason they can't find it is because it's not the gate they're looking for; and it's certainly not the gate the masses choose to enter. Jesus went on to contrast the *narrow gate* with the *wide gate*, saying, "for the gate is wide, and the way is broad that leads to destruction, and many are those who enter by it" (v. 13). The imagery here is obvious: both the narrow and the wide gate have a sign over them saying, "This Way To Heaven." But unlike the narrow gate that is *restrictive*, the wide gate is *gaping, inclusive,* and *attractive*. The idea of "striving" is wholly unnecessary in the wide gate; there's no need for conscious, strenuous effort; no need for groaning, or crying out for mercy. And the "wide . . . way" is the easy way—the way of the world, the way of the unregenerate.

Widening the Gate

Many modern-day pastors bent on attracting "seekers" have learned how to market the wide gate by defining sin in such a way that virtually no one could be offended, and thus eliminate the need for genuine repentance and regeneration. The essence of their definition of sin is basically this: *Sin includes all those things we think and do that rob us of fellowship with God and steal away the happiness He wants us to enjoy*. The good news of the gospel is then reduced to nothing more than *God loving us so much that He sent His Son to save us from our unhappiness*. But describing sin apart from the offended righteousness of God is not just irresponsible, it is damning. Apart from an understanding of man's condemnation that evokes the wrath of God, the gospel is no gospel at all.

This is the sad legacy of the consumer-driven mindset of evangelical pragmatism that makes the *gospel a product* and the *preacher a salesmen*—a concept totally foreign to Scripture. As you might expect, the salesman must make the product appealing to the consumer by presenting it in an atmosphere of entertainment and removing any offense that might prevent the sale. But when the solemnity of the eternal destiny of people's souls is obscured by amusement, and the offense of the cross is removed to overcome resistance, the *appealing* gospel becomes a *different* gospel that damns both those who embrace it and those who preach it (Gal. 1:8). For this reason, Paul said to the Corinthians, "I determined to know nothing among you except Jesus Christ, and Him crucified" (1 Cor. 2:4). And though it was "to Jews a stumbling block and to Gentiles foolishness" (1 Cor. 1:23), he knew his uncompromising proclamation was the only truth that could save, causing him to say, "My message and my preaching were not in persuasive words of wisdom, but in demonstration of the Spirit and of power" (1 Cor. 2:4).

When the average postmodern unbeliever hears a modified gospel presented by a false teacher bent on overcoming resistance—as if he, not God, is sovereign over salvation—the sinner has no basis to grasp the terrifying reality that "the wrath of God abides on him" (John 3:36). Instead, he will respond as follows (consistent with numerous conversations I have had with people in this regard):

> Yeah, if God is real, I suppose I am guilty of ignoring Him. I don't think about God very much, and I love lots of things more than God. So to that extent, I suppose I am living in prideful rebellion. And yes, I have fallen just like the whole Satan analogy—just look at all the junk in my life. Relationships are messed up. My marriage is boring. My finances are a wreck. I hate my job. I basically feel as though my life is going nowhere fast. For sure, I need to be saved from all this stuff. Maybe God is the answer to my unhappiness, my lack of success, my negative emotions, and my lack of purpose and direction in life. I'm just glad God loves me just the way I am, because I'm not sure I could ever change. I am what I am. And I'm not sure why Jesus had to come and die for me (assuming all that's true), but I'm

glad He did, I guess. I sure don't get all that stuff about the Father killing His Son—so much for a loving God. But I'm told I have to accept that stuff by faith, so I guess I will. Nothing else seems to be working. I suppose Jesus died on the cross so He could demonstrate what selfless love is all about. Anyway, I want to take advantage of anything God may have to offer to make my life better. So I think I'll accept Jesus as my personal Savior and see what happens.

Moralistic Therapeutic Deism

Perhaps one of the most graphic manifestations of this kind of unregenerate pseudo-Christian thinking can be seen in the typical "Christian" teenager—a tragedy that also dominates virtually every acre of the landscape of Protestant evangelicalism. Christian Smith and his fellow researchers with the National Study of Youth and Religion at the University of North Carolina at Chapel Hill observed the essence of this danger after conducting more than 3,000 interviews with American adolescents to determine their religious beliefs. There they discovered a deception they identified as "Moralistic Therapeutic Deism," a concept summarized in *Soul Searching: The Religious and Spiritual Eyes of American Teenagers* by Christian Smith with Melinda Lundquist Denton.[17] According to these researchers, Moralistic Therapeutic Deism consists of beliefs like these:

1. "A god exists who created and ordered the world and watches over human life on earth."
2. "God wants people to be good, nice, and fair to each other, as taught in the Bible and by most world religions."
3. "The central goal of life is to be happy and to feel good about oneself."
4. "God does not need to be particularly involved in one's life except when God is needed to resolve a problem."
5. "Good people go to heaven when they die." That, in sum, is the creed to which much adolescent faith can be reduced. . . . When it came to the most crucial questions of faith and beliefs, many adolescents responded with a shrug and "whatever."

As a matter of fact, the researchers. . . found that American teenagers are incredibly inarticulate about their religious beliefs, and most are virtually unable to offer any serious theological understanding. As Smith reports, "To the extent that the teens we interviewed did manage to articulate what they understood and believed religiously, it became clear that most religious teenagers either do not really comprehend what their own religious traditions say they are supposed to believe, or they do understand it and simply do not care to believe it. Either way, it is apparent that most religiously affiliated U.S. teens are not particularly interested in espousing and upholding the beliefs of their faith traditions, or that their communities of faith are failing in attempts to educate their youth, or both."

As the researchers explained, "For most teens, nobody has to do anything in life, including anything to do with religion. 'Whatever' is just fine, if that's what a person wants."[18]

What a radically different attitude and response to that of the tax collector in Luke 18 who, when confronted with his sin, was so overwhelmed with guilt and unworthiness that he "was even unwilling to lift up his eyes to heaven, but was beating his breast, saying, 'God, be merciful to me, the sinner!'" (v. 13). This is certainly evidence of regeneration that will yield the fruits of genuine repentance. What a blessed thing it is to behold the Holy Spirit awakening souls to the truth of their sin and their Savior! And when fully awakened, such people will forsake everything to enter in through the narrow gate of genuine repentance.

In Luke 16:16, Jesus warned that when "the gospel of the kingdom of God is preached . . . everyone is forcing his way into it." This denotes a vigorous, forceful pressing into the kingdom. Jesus expanded upon this concept warning that "from the days of John the Baptist until now the kingdom of heaven suffers violence, and violent men take it by force" (Matt. 11:12). There, Jesus emphasized that, despite the world's relentless opposition to the kingdom of God, it will never be subdued by the wickedness of men or the power of Satan. And those who, by the power of regenerating grace that energizes faith, see their sin and love the Savior will forcefully press their way into the kingdom, even if it costs them their life.

So Jesus presses His followers to choose between two options both claiming "This way to heaven!" They must choose between two gates: the *narrow* and the *wide*, and between two ways: the *narrow* and the *broad*. The world will hate those who enter in through the narrow, but love those who chose the wide. Saints will suffer on the narrow way, but those who are "Christians" in name only will fit right in with the rest of the unregenerate on the broad way. True believers will *serve Christ* on the narrow way, but the unsaved will *serve self* and "[their] father the devil" (John 8:44) on the broad.

Sadly, much of the church today is made up of *wide gate, broad way* "Christians" who are externally religious, and even claim to be "born again," but who have no saving understanding of the true gospel and have not wholeheartedly embraced Christ in repentant faith. For example, one in four born-again "Christians" embraces universalist beliefs when it comes to salvation, according to a Barna analysis of trend data. Twenty-five percent of born-again Christians said all people are eventually saved or accepted by God. A similar proportion, 26 percent, said a person's religion does not matter because all faiths teach the same lessons. And an even higher proportion, 40 percent, of born-again Christians said they believe Christians and Muslims worship the same God. Barna defined universalism as the belief that all human beings will eventually be saved after death. The California-based research and polling firm defines born-again Christians as people who have made "a personal commitment to Jesus Christ that is still important in their life today, and who believe they will go to heaven after death because they confessed their sins and accepted Jesus

Christ as their savior."[19] But sadly, given the heresy many believe, they will one day learn otherwise.

The Dire Warning

In light of this, Jesus offers the most horrifying prediction ever made concerning the masses of people who fall prey to self-deception and believe they have been raised from spiritual death to spiritual life and reconciled God through faith in His Son, the Lord Jesus Christ, when in fact, they have not. He said, "Not everyone who says to Me, 'Lord, Lord,' will enter the kingdom of heaven, but he who does the will of My Father who is in heaven will enter" (Matt. 7:21). What a terrifying thought! This is one of the most sobering passages in Scripture—one that describes the horrifying climax of self-deception. Here the masquerade of the *many* who entered the *wide gate* and traveled the *broad way* is exposed.

The prophetic lament, "Lord, Lord," that Jesus describes is haunting—one that indicates they will have a perceived zeal and devotion to Christ. They will honestly believe that their profession and conduct were certain proof that they were followers of Christ. It is important to note that Jesus is not necessarily referring to heretics, agnostics, atheists, apostates, or pagans, but to those who profess faith in

Him. They will call Him Lord. But obviously, not all who *profess* Him actually *possess* Him. A man's profession alone is meaningless unless it is validated by a selfless life devoted to Christ—the inevitable manifestation of the new birth! True believers are "[known] by their fruits" (Matt. 7:20), not by their profession of allegiance to Christ. For this reason, Jesus went on to say, "Not everyone who says to Me, 'Lord, Lord,' will enter the kingdom of heaven; *but he who does the will of My father who is in heaven*" (v. 21; emphasis mine).

Their ignorance of this most fundamental truth can be seen in the contrast of Jesus' use of the words "says" rather than "does" in verse 21. Here the old adage "What we do speaks louder than words" is most fitting. To be sure, talk is cheap. Therefore, obedience is the only reliable indicator of one's faith in Christ. What validates spiritual rebirth and genuine saving faith is *doing the will of the Father* (v. 21).

Now, it is important to point out that we don't *earn* our salvation by faith *plus* works. That is the damning heresy of a false gospel, like we see in the Roman Catholic church that teaches justification is a result of *faith plus works; grace plus merit; through Christ plus other mediators; by Scripture plus tradition; for the glory of God plus Mary and other saints.* This is why there was a Protestant Reformation (1517–

1648). The Reformers taught the true gospel whose basic theological principles are summarized in the *Five Solas* (five Latin phrases or slogans):

- *Sola Fide*, by faith alone.
- *Sola Scriptura*, by Scripture alone.
- *Solus Christus*, through Christ alone.
- *Sola Gratia*, by grace alone.
- *Soli Deo Gloria*, glory to God alone.

The true gospel teaches that works don't *earn* salvation; they *prove* it (James 2:17). Jesus said, "If you abide in My Word, then you are truly disciples of Mine" (John 8:31). Works are never the *root* of justification by faith; they are the *fruit* of it. The apostle John writes,

> The one who says, "I have come to know Him," and does not keep His commandments, is a liar, and the truth is not in him; but whoever keeps His word, in him the love of God has truly been perfected. By this we know that we are in Him; the one who says he abides in Him ought himself to walk in the same manner as He walked.
> (1 John 2:3–6)

This describes a life pattern of Christlike obedience to the will of God energized by the miracle of the new birth; otherwise, ". . . faith, if it has no works, is dead, being by itself" (James 2:17).

Once again, in Matthew 7, Jesus makes it clear that the majority of those who profess Him as Lord are *self-deceived*, proven by lives that did not demonstrate their professed allegiance to Him. Unlike the *few*, the *many* "do not do the will of the Father who is in heaven"—a sheer impossibility apart from the regenerating work of the Holy Spirit. They professed Christ with their lips but not with their lives, because they were still spiritually "dead in [their] trespasses and sins" (Eph. 2:1).

The Dubious Defense

Jesus went on to describe the *dubious defense* of the self-deceived—those who masqueraded as His disciples by performing religious works and making orthodox declarations of faith without any heartfelt love for Christ or commitment to obey His will. In perhaps the most alarming words in all of Scripture, Jesus describes the terrifying dialogue in this coming hour of judgment, saying,

> Many will say to Me on that day, "Lord, Lord, did we not prophesy in Your name, and in Your name cast out demons, and in Your name perform many miracles?"
>
> And then I will declare to them, "I never knew you; depart from Me, you who practice lawlessness."
> (Matt. 7:22–23)

The eschatological scene is one of unspeakable incredulity and terror. The damned are dumfounded! They can't believe they're standing before the Lord Jesus Christ not as their *Savior* and *Lord*, but as their *Judge* and *Executioner*. In desperation the "many" will plead their case, but to no avail; and in an effort to demonstrate their submission to His sovereign rule, they will address Him with a perfunctory, "Lord, Lord." They will argue their case enthusiastically by supplying outward signs of devotion to Christ and His church, including what they considered to be miraculous gifts of the Holy Spirit such as *prophecies*, *exorcisms*, and various other kinds of *miracles* (v. 22)—counterfeit signs and wonders that can be fabricated by human chicanery and demonic influence (*cf.* Acts 19:13–16; Rev. 13:13–14). But the penetrating eye of divine omniscience will see the truth. Then Jesus will say, "I never knew you," indicating that even those with the most sincere profession of faith will be sent away to destruction if they entered the *wide gate* and traversed the *broad way* of the worldly masses who were Christian in name only.

What a contrast to the *narrow gate* that demands self-denial and repentance produced by regeneration—the gate of genuine saving faith that requires people to give up all that they *are* and *have* to follow Christ. This is the gate of the "few" who are "humble and contrite of spirit, and who tremble at [His] word" (Isa. 66:2); those who "mourn" over their sin (Matt. 5:4) and "hunger and thirst for righteousness" (v. 6); those who seek the one true Lord with all their heart (Jer. 29:13).

But the "Christless" Christians of the *wide gate* and the *broad way* will be those who served a god of their own liking and making—one that appealed to their fallen flesh, one they were convinced would accept them on their terms. Therefore, what they *say* will not match what they *did*—an accusation consistent with Jesus' rebuke in Luke 6:46 when He said: "Why do you call Me, 'Lord, Lord,' and do not do what I say?" This will be the dreadful end of the unregenerate that were never raised from spiritual death to spiritual life (John 3:6). John MacArthur described it this way:

The repentant life will be a changed life. The primary message of John's first epistle is that the truly redeemed life will manifest itself in a transformed life, in which confession of sin (1:8–10), obedience to God's will (2:4–6), love of God's other children (2:9–11; 3:16–17), and practice of righteousness (3:4–10) are normal and habitual. "By this is My Father glorified, that you bear much fruit, and so prove to be My disciples" (John 15:8). Anything less is damning demon-faith (James 2:19) that is orthodox but fruitless.[20]

Sadly, the absence of spiritual fruit is one of the most defining characteristics of modern evangelicalism. While worldliness and doctrinal compromise are major contributors to this barrenness, the greatest corruptor is the massive number of unregenerate professing Christians who make up the church today. It is no wonder the church has so little spiritual authority and influence on the culture. Jesus warned of this when He said,

> You are the salt of the earth; but if the salt has become tasteless, how can it be made salty again? It is no longer good for anything, except to be thrown out and trampled under

foot by men. You are the light of the world. A city set on a hill cannot be hidden; nor does anyone light a lamp and put it under a basket, but on the lampstand, and it gives light to all who are in the house. Let your light shine before men in such a way that they may see your good works, and glorify your Father who is in heaven.
(Matt. 5:13–16)

Instead of being "the salt of the earth" that slows down the decay and corruption of society and preserves that which is true and holy, "the salt has become tasteless," unable to oppose corruption, unable to influence society as a moral antiseptic, unable to provide a taste of godliness in a world that knows so little of it. Unfortunately, such a church is "no longer good for anything, except to be thrown out and trampled under foot by men" (v. 13) — and that is precisely what we see happening to the church today. Furthermore, instead of the church being "the light of the world" that illumines the darkness with the dazzling light of the gospel and the radiant beams of righteousness — the very purpose of our redemption — it now contributes to the darkness with its prosperity-cult charlatans, entertainment-driven ministries, and culturally driven gospel distortions that are purposefully *humanitarian* rather than *redemptive*.

The pseudo-Christianity in our culture continues to be fertile soil for the seeds of depravity to germinate and grow into a harvest of unimaginable and unrestrained moral degeneracy in our country. Satanic lies and diabolical political movements are now so rampant in the United States of America that it has become obvious to any rational observer that our nation is descending into an abyss of lawless anarchy from which there may be no recovery. And much of the blame can be placed on false teachers and undiscerning pastors who refuse to confront sin and its effects with the only truth that can save, like the wicked leaders of ancient Judah that God rebuked through His servant Jeremiah saying,

> "They have healed the brokenness of My people superficially, saying, 'Peace, peace,' but there is no peace. Were they ashamed because of the abomination they have done? They were not even ashamed at all; they did not even know how to blush. Therefore they shall fall among those who fall; at the time that I punish them, they shall be cast down," says the Lord.
> (Jer. 6:14–15)

The Damning Sentence

I cannot imagine a statement that can even remotely compare to Jesus' horrifying pronouncement, "I never knew you; depart from Me, you who practice lawlessness" (Matt. 7:23). Jesus' use of the word "knew" (*ginōskō*) was a Hebrew idiom denoting an intimate, loving relationship, often used to describe marital intimacy (see Gen. 4:1, 17; etc.; where "had relations" is literally "knew," as in the KJV).[21] We see this in Jesus' declaration: "My sheep hear My voice, and I know them" (John 10:27).

The Lord of the church to whom has been given "all authority . . . in heaven and on earth" (Matt. 28:18) will see through the external religious veneer of the hypocrites who entered the *wide gate* and traveled the *broad way* of the *many* rather than the *few* and say, "depart from Me, you who practice lawlessness" (v. 23b)—the grammar of the phrase indicating continuous, habitual actions. And indeed, this is the heart pattern of the unregenerate. Their life-dominating motivations and their secret desires are self-willed and rebellious against God, despite their outward religiosity. Later we read our Lord's haunting words: " . . . and his house fell, and great was its fall" (v. 27b).

Such will be the damning sentence of the unregenerate who professed Him with their lips, but not with their lives, those who "did not receive the love of the truth so as to be saved" (2 Thess. 2:10).

4

Evidence of Regeneration

If anyone is in Christ, he is a new creature; the old things passed away; behold, new things have come.
2 Corinthians 5:17

As we have seen thus far, one of Satan's most clever devices is tricking people into believing they have been reconciled to God and are heaven bound when, in fact, they're not. While he accomplishes this through a variety of false teachings, I fear the altar call system of evangelism is especially vulnerable to this criticism. At the conclusion of many church services and evangelistic crusades, people are given an invitation to respond to a gospel message (often distorted) by raising their hand, walking an aisle, and repeating a prayer—whereupon they will immediately be welcomed into the kingdom of God without any evidence to validate whether or not they have truly been made a "new creature" in Christ and "new things have come" (2 Cor. 5:17). Worse yet, with no opportunity for the seed of the gospel to bear the fruit of genuine repentance, they are told to never let anyone tell them their salvation is not sure.

This method of evangelism poses a serious danger. When immediate external acts in response to evangelistic appeals are considered evidence of new birth instead of a changed life, those who may be "accepting Jesus as their personal Savior" for all the wrong reasons will be deceived into believing they are born again. Furthermore, when a non-offensive gospel that appeals to carnal minds is preached and then embraced by the masses who love it, the perceived success of a hybrid gospel seed guaranteed to grow in any soil will quickly gain popularity and fill churches with unholy tares that will choke out the wheat.

This is what happens, according to British preacher and biblical commentator, Thomas Scott (1747–1821), when

> You make up a plausible gospel, calculated to humour the pride, soothe the consciences, engage the hearts, and raise the affection of natural men, who love nobody but them-

selves. . . . What wonder if, when it is evidently calculated to fill the unrenewed mind with false confidence and joy, it has this effect? What wonder if, when the true character of God is unknown, and a false character of him is framed in the fancy—a God all love and no justice, very fond of such believers, as his favourites—they have very warm affections towards him? . . . I cannot but avow my fears that Satan has propagated much of this false religion, among many widely different classes of religious professors; and it shines so brightly in the types of numbers, who "take all for gold that glitters," that, unless the fallacy be detected, it bids fair to be the prevailing religion in many places.[22]

Charles Finney and Altar Call Evangelism

Sadly, this is the tragic legacy of the errant Arminian (even, Pelagian) theology of the flamboyant revivalist preacher Charles G. Finney (1792–1875) that has been adopted by many evangelicals over the years. According to Iain Murray, Finney believed "human depravity is 'voluntary' condition, that is to say, its continuance depends upon the choice of the human will. (Finney said) 'Let a man once decide for Christ and he will become a new man.' So the evangelist is not simply to preach Christ and to tell men of their duty to believe; he has to help *make* that believing a reality by appointing some outward action to *assist* a change of will."[23] Murray goes on to say that Finney

> believed that evangelism has to involve telling gospel hearers that they are able to become Christians at once: they have to be presented with an immediate choice, and to show the sincerity and reality of their choosing Christ let them do something to prove it. Hence what became known as the "altar call", that is, the practice of calling those who would be converted to take some visible action which would clinch the matter. The fact that such novel public actions were calculated to create natural excitement was the opposite, in Finney's mind, to being a drawback: "God has found it necessary to take advantage of the excitability there is in mankind to produce powerful excitements among them before he can lead them to obey."[24]

Obviously, this method of evangelism based upon a foreign gospel that has no dependency on sovereign grace alone will produce many false converts. In 1838, Joseph Ives Foot, a Presbyterian minister who lived in that era and witnessed the results of Finney's ministry wrote this:

> During ten years, hundreds, and perhaps thousands, were annually reported to be converted on all hands; but now it is admitted, that his [Finney's] real converts are comparatively few. It is declared even by himself, that "the great body of them are a disgrace to religion."[25]

Writing in 1835 in the *Princeton Essays*, Albert B. Dod made a similar observation:

> Appearances were somewhat in favour of the new measures. At least wherever they were carried, converts were multiplied. But it is now generally understood that the numerous converts of the new measures have been, in most cases, like the morning cloud and the early dew. In some places, not a half, a fifth, or even a tenth part of them remain.[26]

Someone has well stated that *the one thing we learn from history is that we never learn from history*. This is certainly true in this regard. Countless people have responded to emotional invitations without ever really understanding the true gospel and their desperate need for saving grace. Nevertheless, as Michael Horton has aptly stated,

> The New York revivalist was the oft-quoted and celebrated champion of the Christian singer Keith Green and the Youth With A Mission organization. He is particularly esteemed among the leaders of the Christian Right and the Christian Left, by both Jerry Falwell and Jim Wallis (Sojourners' magazine), and his imprint can be seen in movements that appear to be diverse, but in reality are merely heirs to Finney's legacy. From the Vineyard movement and the Church Growth Movement to the political and social crusades, televangelism, and the Promise Keepers movement, as a former Wheaton College president rather glowingly cheered, "Finney, lives on!"

That is because Finney's moralistic impulse envisioned a church that was in large measure an agency of personal and social reform rather than the institution in which the means of grace, Word and Sacrament, are made available to believers who then take the Gospel to the world. In the nineteenth century, the evangelical movement became increasingly identified with political causes—from abolition of slavery and child labor legislation to women's rights and the prohibition of alcohol. In a desperate effort at regaining this institutional power and the glory of "Christian America" (a vision that is always powerful in the imagination, but, after the disintegration of Puritan New England, elusive), the turn-of-the century Protestant establishment launched moral campaigns to "Americanize" immigrants, enforce moral instruction and "character education." Evangelists pitched their American gospel in terms of its practical usefulness to the individual and the nation.[27]

While Finney's theology was errant on many levels (beyond the purpose of our discussion), his denial of the doctrine of original sin and man's utter inability to contribute to his salvation because of the bondage of his sinful nature is in direct contradiction to the doctrine of regeneration. After all, who needs the Spirit if a preacher can get someone to make a decision on his own and cause himself to be born again? And by what standard of measure can one be called a Christian if all that is necessary is for a man to decide on his own to make a decision for Christ (with the help of a compelling evangelist) and then validate his conversion solely on the basis of an external act and profession? Herein is the deceptive legacy of a theological system and methodology that not only ignores the doctrines of regeneration and justification, but is also in conflict with them.

Evidence of the New Birth

When, through the power of the revealed Word of God, the Spirit moves upon a sinner's heart and causes him to be "born again" (John 3:3, 7), the supernatural gift of faith is suddenly imparted. Spiritually blinded eyes can suddenly see the light of Christ's glory (2 Cor. 4:4–6; *cf.* John 3:3; Heb. 11:1), making the sinner's perception of light (regeneration) the *cause*, not the *effect* of faith. For indeed, spiritual cadavers in a state of spiritual death (Eph. 2:1–3) whose minds are "hostile toward God and cannot subject [themselves] to the law of God" (Rom. 8:7) are utterly incapable of understanding the things of the Spirit, much less embracing them in repentant faith (1 Cor. 2:14). In 1 John 5:4, the apostle writes, "For everyone who has been born of God overcomes the world. And this is the victory that has overcome the world—our faith." Similarly, Jesus told Nicodemus, "Unless one is born again he cannot see the kingdom of God" (John 3:3).

With the new birth, Christ is miraculously formed in the heart (Gal. 4:2) and the newborn saint is "renewed to a true knowledge according to the image of the One who created him" (Col. 3:10)—just as God had predestined in eternity past (Rom. 8:29). Sinners become saints and are suddenly made partakers of the divine nature (2 Peter 1:4), causing them to bear a resemblance of the image of God. Warfield defined regeneration as the

> radical and complete transformation wrought in the soul (Rom. 12:12; Eph. 4:23) by God the Holy Spirit (Titus 3:5; Eph. 4:23), by virtue of which we become "new men" (Eph. 4:24; Col. 3:9), but in knowledge and holiness of truth created after the image of God (Eph. 4:24; Col. 3:10; Rom. 12:2).[28]

I was deeply moved the first time I read London theologian and pastor, John Gill's (1697–1771) contrast between the new birth (second birth) and the first birth (physical birth). His insights into Scripture are compelling and encouraging to every believer who will readily identify with his comparisons:

The first birth is of sinful parents, and in their image; the second birth is of God, and in his image; the first birth is of corruptible, the second birth of incorruptible seed; the first birth is in sin, the second birth is in holiness and righteousness; by the first birth men are polluted and unclean, by the second birth they become holy and commence to be saints; the first birth is of the flesh and is carnal, the second birth is of the Spirit and is spiritual, and makes men spiritual men; by the first birth men are foolish and unwise, being born like a wild ass's colt; by the second birth they become knowing and wise unto salvation: by the first birth they are slaves to sin and the lusts of the flesh, are home born slaves; by the second birth they become Christ's free men. . . . A regenerate man breathes in prayer to God, and pants after him; after more knowledge of him in Christ, after communion with him, after the discoveries of his love. . . . There are, in a regenerate man, which shows that he is made alive, cravings after spiritual food: as soon as an infant is born, it shows motions for its mother's milk, after the breast: so newborn babes desire the sincere milk of the word, that they may grow thereby. They have their spiritual sense exercised about spiritual objects . . . they feel the burden of sin on their consciences; the workings of the Spirit of God in their hearts . . . which makes it a plain case that they are alive; a dead man feels nothing.[29]

The Spirit-wrought transformation in the soul causes a man to see the dreadful condition of his sinful heart and the underserved mercy, grace, and love of Christ that he now embraces in saving faith. Though we "formerly lived in the lusts of our flesh, indulging the desires of the flesh and of the mind, and were by nature children of wrath" the Spirit "made us alive together with Christ" (Eph. 2:3, 5). At the moment of our new birth, we are made new creatures in Christ, setting into motion a process of sanctification what will culminate in Christlikeness, for "that which is born of the flesh is flesh, and what which is born of the Spirit is spirit" (John 3:6; John 1:13; 1 Peter 1:23). The life of the newborn saint is characterized by overcoming the wicked influences of Satan's world system (1 John 5:4)—including a newfound hatred for what he or she once loved, and a love for what he or she once hated. The Spirit plants within us new desires, loves, passions, inclinations, beliefs, and values (2 Cor. 5:17) so that we manifest the fruit of the Spirit: "love, joy, peace, patience, kindness, goodness, faithfulness, gentleness, self-control" (Gal. 5:22–23). Wayne Grudem adds this helpful insight:

> Related to this kind of fruit is another kind of fruit—the results of one's life and ministry as they have influence on others and on the church. There are some people who profess to be Christians but whose influence on others is to discourage them, to drag them down, to injure their faith, and to provoke controversy and divisiveness. The result of their life and ministry is not to build up others and to build up the church, but to tear it down. On the other hand, there are those who seem to edify others in every conversation, every prayer, and every work of ministry they put their hand to. Jesus said, regarding false prophets, "You will know them by their fruits. . . . Every sound tree bears good fruit, but the bad tree bears evil fruit. . . . Thus you will know them by their fruits" (Matt. 7:16–20).[30]

With the disposition of the soul radically changed, God's desires become our desires (Ps. 37:4) and He causes us "to become obedient from the heart to that form of teaching to which [we] were committed" (Rom. 6:17; *cf.* 1 John 2:23–24), for indeed, "If you know that He is righteous, you know that everyone also who practices righteousness is born of Him" (1 John 2:29).

Having been delivered from the power of sin and the penalty of the law, "the requirement of the law is fulfilled in us," according to Romans 8:4, "who do not walk according to the flesh, but according to the Spirit, though the body is dead because of sin, yet our spirit is alive because of His righteousness." And as the newly implanted seed of divine life begins to germinate and bear fruit, the Spirit uses the Word of God to grow us into the likeness of Christ (1 Peter 1:23), causing us to constantly be putting to death the principle of sin that remains incarcerated in our unredeemed humanness (Rom. 7:14–25) through the habitual and joyful putting away of reoccurring manifestations of sin and putting on patterns of righteousness (Eph. 4:22–24).

Evidence of regeneration will also include an intimate love for Christ that animates a personal pursuit of holiness that includes a longing for personal fellowship with Him through prayer and worship (John 15:4, 7), a love for other believers (1 John 3:14), and a subjective awareness of the love of God and the Spirit's leading in our life in obedience to the will of God (Rom. 8:15–16; *cf.* 1 John 4:13).

As every twice-born saint will attest, the miracle of spiritual sight wrought within the soul by the power of the Holy Spirit will set into motion the most soul-satisfying and soul-exhilarating realities known to man, but not to any man, for this is only available to those who, by the regenerating power of sovereign grace, place their trust in the Lord Jesus Christ as the only hope of their salvation. I pray this is true of you. If so, together we, with full-throated praise, can join the apostle Paul in saying. . .

> For I am confident of this very thing, that He who began a good work in you will perfect it until the day of Christ Jesus.
> (Phil. 1:6)

> Now to Him who is able to do far more abundantly beyond all that we ask or think, according to the power that works within us, to Him be the glory in the church and in Christ Jesus to all generations forever and ever. Amen.
> (Eph. 3:20–21)

Endnotes

1 https://bible.org/article/hound-heaven#P15_2097

2 R. Kent Hughes, *1001 Great Stories and Quotes* (Wheaton, IL: Tyndale, 1998), 393–94.

3 John MacArthur and Richard Mayhue, General Editors, *Biblical Doctrine: A Systematic Summary of Bible Truth* (Crossway, Wheaton, Illinois, 2017), 580.

4 https://www.spurgeongems.org/sermon/chs1977.pdf

5 David Dickson, *Select Practical Writings of David Dickson, Vol. 1* (Edinburgh: Printed for the Assemblies Committee, 1845), 211.

6 https://www.thekingdomcollective.com/spurgeon/sermon/3121/

7 https://hilltopbiblechurch.org/2019/06/01/living-in-dangerous-times-part-13/

8 https://pulpitandpen.org/2019/07/03/bethel-church-weirdos-still-grave-sucking/

9 Eric J. Alexander, *Our Great God and Saviour* (Edinburgh: The Banner of Truth Trust, 2010), 72).

10 Spurgeon sermon: *The Fourfold Treasure*, Sermon #991, delivered April 27, 1871. https://www.spurgeongems.org/vols16-18/chs991.pdf

11 Iain H. Murray, *Evangelicalism Divided: A Record of Crucial Change in the Years 1950 to 2000* (Edinburgh, UK, The Banner of Truth Trust, 2000), 69.

12 Horatius Bonar, *God's Morning: or, Thoughts on Genesis* (London: Nisbet, 1875), 365-6.

13 Iain H. Murray, *Evangelicalism Divided: A Record of*

Crucial Change in the Years 1950 to 2000 (Banner of Truth Trust, Edinburgh, 2000), 254–55.

14   Iain H. Murray, *Evangelicalism Divided* (Edinburgh: The Banner of Truth Trust, 2000), 313.

15   John Fast: https://hilltopbiblechurch.org/2019/06/01/living-in-dangerous-times-part-13/

16   Nolland, J. (2005). *The Gospel of Matthew: A Commentary on the Greek Text* (p. 332). Grand Rapids, MI; Carlisle: W.B. Eerdmans; Paternoster Press.

17   https://www.christianpost.com/news/moralistic-therapeutic-deism-the-new-american-religion.html

18   Ibid.

19   http://www.christianpost.com/news/many-born-again-christians-hold-universalist-view-barna-finds-49883/#MOf0DZqyPXOroJUh.99

20   John F. MacArthur, *Matthew 1–7: The MacArthur New Testament Commentary*, (Chicago: Moody, 1985), 454.

21   Ibid., 479.

22   Thomas Scott, *Letter and Papers, ed. John Scott* (London: Seeley, 1824), 441-4.

23   Iain H. Murray, *Pentecost Today? The Biblical Basis for Understanding Revival* (Edinburgh, The Banner of Truth Trust, Reprinted 2017), 39.

24   Ibid., 42–43.

25   Iain H. Murray, *Revival and Revivalism: The Making and Marring of American Evangelicalism 1750-1858* (Edinburgh: The Banner of Truth Trust, Reprinted 1996), 289.

26   Ibid., 46.

27   https://www.monergism.com/disturbing-legacy-charles-finney

28 B. B. Warfield, *Biblical and Theological Studies* (Philadelphia, PA; Presbyterian & Reformed Publications, 1952), 351.

29 https://www.monergism.com/thethreshold/sdg/gill/A_Body_of_Doctrinal_Divinity_-_John_Gill.pdf

30 Wayne Grudem, *Systematic Theology: An Introduction to Biblical Doctrine* (Zondervan Publishing House, Grand Rapids, Michigan, 1994), 804.